Rational Decisionmaking
in
Higher Education

About the Author

Ellen Earle Chaffee is a senior associate in the NCHEMS Organizational Studies Program. Her current research interests, in addition to models of organizational decisionmaking, include the role of strategy in college and university management and effective approaches to planning and budgeting. Dr. Chaffee holds a Ph.D. in administration and policy analysis from Stanford University. Her administrative responsibilities during 10 years at Stanford and North Dakota State Universities included budget development, equal opportunity, and student affairs administration. She has also taught at the University of Colorado School of Business and has been active in consulting, speaking, and serving on national and state boards. Her most recent work at NCHEMS deals with strategies for private liberal arts colleges to recover from financial decline.

 An NCHEMS Executive Overview

Rational Decisionmaking
in
Higher Education

Ellen Earle Chaffee

1983

National Center for Higher Education Management Systems
P.O. Box P   Boulder, Colorado 80302
An Affirmative Action/Equal Opportunity Employer

LB2341
.C47
1983

Published in 1983 in the United States of America by the
National Center for Higher Education Management Systems,
Inc., Boulder, Colorado 80302

Printed in the United States of America. This publication was
not printed at the expense of the federal government.

Designed by Grant Duncan,
Graphic Directions, Boulder, Colorado

iv

Contents

Chapter 1
Five Models of Organizational
Decisionmaking . . . .

The Decision Process, the Rational
Model, the Collegial Model, the
Political Model, the Bureaucratic
Model, Organized Anarchy

CONTENTS

List of Tables

List of Figures

Acknowledgments

I extend special thanks to Joan Knapp for her imaginative editorial assistance. I also appreciate the helpful comments received from Dane Cox, Carol Guardo, Fred Harcleroad, John Hopkins, Bill Johnston, Pat Lemp, Jennifer Presley, Ted Tedesco, and John Wittstruck. And I thank many others at Stanford, the University of Colorado, and 19 colleges and universities to whom I've promised anonymity—they were, without exception, gracious, candid, and patient.

The research described in chapter 2 was supported by the Bush Foundation and by the Institute for Research on Educational Finance and Governance at Stanford.

Introduction

During the second week of May 1982, Assistant Professor Jose Arguelles received two communications from the University of Colorado: (1) he had been selected by students as Teacher of the Year at CU's Denver campus, and (2) he would not be granted tenure because his research did not conform to the university's standards. Predictably, area newspapers played up the story, students labeled the nontenure decision "unfair," and minority groups labeled it "prejudiced." However, the regents' criteria for awarding tenure, which include demonstrated competence in teaching and scholarly work, were well known to the faculty. Arguelles did not claim to have met the traditional definition of scholarly work while at CU. Rather, he contended that teaching skills should count for more in the decision and that the traditional definition of scholarly work was too narrow. While Arguelles and his supporters disagreed about the university's priorities, they had to admit that a decision that on the surface might seem capricious and even counterproductive was at least consistent with the stated values of the university. Thus, they did not appeal the decision.

This scenario may have occurred on many campuses in 1982; in view of shrinking enrollments and funds, it may occur even more frequently during the rest of the decade. Moreover, as faculty become increasingly anxious to secure tenure while administrators continue to seek the flexibility that comes from not awarding it, charges of capricious and prejudiced decisions by administrators may be leveled and substantiated by faculty.

Tension between faculty and administrators is indeed unfortunate, but the thesis of this book is that when controversial decisions affecting an institution's achievement of important goals must be made, tension can be lessened and polarity avoided if all parties involved in the decision understand the process of decisionmaking and feel assured that this process is rational. Furthermore, when rational decisions and the conditions that make rational decisions possible consistently characterize a college or university, that institution experiences not only a high proportion of excellent decisions but also a high degree of confidence in itself, in its values, and in its administration.

What is a "rational" decision and how does it differ from other kinds of decisions? I define the process of rational decisionmaking as a conscious choice made by a central authority among simultaneously displayed alternatives. The choice must be based on previously recognized values and on evidence that the alternative will, in fact, result in the realization of these values. Thus, the decision not to grant tenure to Professor Arguelles could be judged "rational" only within the larger context of the university's values as expressed in its stated goals. This necessary connection with values gives authority both to the decision and the decisionmaker.

A controversial issue in higher-education literature is whether the rational model is feasible and, if so, whether it is preferable to other models of decisionmaking. Indeed, all previously published empirical research that describes decisionmaking at colleges and universities argues that the process is not rational in the sense that I have defined that term, but rather falls into other categories, which may be compared with the rational as follows:

INTRODUCTION

1. Rational: directed by values, based on supporting data
2. Collegial: directed by consensus
3. Political: directed by conflicting self-interests and power
4. Bureaucratic: directed by traditional administrative patterns
5. Anarchical: directed by accidents of timing and interest

In practice, a decision process is not likely to follow the pattern of any single model. From one perspective, the process may seem largely collegial, from another, political. However, the models are useful analytic devices that serve as templates through which decision processes may be categorized, understood, and evaluated. Although our focus is on the likely benefits of the rational model, the concept of rationality is clearer when contrasted with alternative concepts, each of which has a useful role to play under appropriate circumstances. Therefore, I will describe each of the five models in detail in chapter 1.

With that background, chapter 2 presents a case study of the rational model as seen in the budget process at Stanford University. Although most higher-education institutions are not major research universities, as Stanford is, the budget problem varies only in its details from one institution to another. Also, most people would agree that budgeting is a decision process in which matching a decision with institutional values and goals is a top priority. When that match is important, the rational model is more suitable than any other.

In chapter 3, I discuss several issues for administrators who are interested in increasing the organization's rational decision-making. Such administrators should be aware of the need for certain organizational conditions that make rational decisions possible—a firm definition of values, a sense of stability, and consistency in decisionmaking. They must also be alert to the issue of centralization/decentralization and to the differences among strategic, tactical, and operational decisions. I point out that while strategic decisions should be structured on the rational model, which requires central authority, they may also be decentralized through broad participation in the decisionmaking process, if such participation is entered into in good faith.

Why should administrators be interested in using or even learning about models of decisionmaking? Consider an analogy. Two teams are competing at basketball. The members of each team are equally athletic and equally intelligent. But the members of one team know the rules, and the members of the other do not. Lacking such basic knowledge as how many points are given for a basket or what behavior is illegal, these players' behavior will be unpredictable, and it will take them a long time to discover the effectiveness of the hook shot. Also, since they lack such concepts as "zone defense" to describe what they are doing, they will have difficulty communicating with each other and learning when one maneuver will be more effective than another. The team that knows the rules, on the other hand, has conceptual tools that enable it to formulate effective strategy.

Similarly, participants in a decisionmaking process need conceptual tools to analyze and modify their organizational behavior. They should be able to recognize what kind of decision process will be most effective for a specific decision opportunity so that they can take steps to encourage the use of the process they believe will be best. When the result is unsatisfactory, they will understand why and be able to make appropriate changes in the decisionmaking structure itself.

This book explains the decisionmaking process in simple, nontechnical language. It promotes the thesis that the use of the rational model, combined with knowledge of other models, can effect significant improvements in management. Underlying this thesis is the premise that, because rational decisions are necessarily connected with values and this connection promotes predictability and fairness, using a rational decision process is a means of saving faculty and students from cynicism, possibly the greatest threat faced by higher education in the 1980s.

Five Models of Organizational Decisionmaking

A t the outset, let us distinguish the specific area of decisionmaking to which this discussion will be confined. Decisionmaking itself is a vast subject, embracing such disciplines as economics, operations research, philosophy, political science, psychology, sociology, and business policy. As an activity, it takes place at various levels—individual, collective, group, and organizational—and it involves such diverse variables as the cognitive capabilities of the decisionmaker's mind, the communication of ideas and values among individuals, and the mathematical calculations that are intended to identify the optimal choice. I will not attempt to deal with this array of factors in this paper; rather, I will confine this study to the process of decisionmaking at the organizational level of analysis. I will deal with interactions that take place over time and that lead the organization to select one course of action in preference to others.

Theorists who have observed such interactions in organizational decisionmaking have noted certain patterns of assumptions and behaviors that seem to appear together. Five such patterns have become widely known as organizational decision models: collegial, bureaucratic, political, anarchical, and rational. Not all of these models are widely accepted as true reflections of organizational behavior, however. The rational model is often criticized as unrealistic. Nevertheless many people who have made this criticism, and virtually everyone who engages in planning, believe that rational decisionmaking is the ideal form. The thesis of this presentation is that the rational model does in fact occur and can be used to advantage by administrators.

Administrators tend to be apprehensive of management theories because these seem to be overly complex and applied only after action is taken. Also, administrators believe that such theories do not reflect an administrator's individual management style. As complex abstractions, theories seem unrealistic and cumbersome. Administrators are too busy making a never-ending stream of decisions to analyze past decisions, and they may see no good reason to do so. General models may seem particularly useless since administrators feel that their personal decision processes are essentially rational yet must be modified to suit each specific situation.

To these objections I will make three counterclaims. First, although models may seem both complex and abstract, they have been shown to reflect reality. Second, analysis of the ways in which organizations make decisions, as distinct from the decisions themselves, can be very useful. And third, decision theories at the organizational level of analysis deal with quite different phenomena than decision theories at the individual level, and these phenomena can be structured in the organization so that they promote a desired decision process regardless of the specific situation.

The first point, complexity, seems to arise because real decision processes often exhibit elements from several models. Thus, for example, in chapter 2 we will see in the midst of the rational

Stanford budget process strong elements of the bureaucratic model, because much of any budget, including Stanford's, is composed of the previous year's base plus an automatic increment. Also, the theories seem to include more elements within each of them than a real process shows—the process may have some elements of one model, some of another, and some that seem to correspond to no model. Life simply is not as tidy as the models imply, and so they seem overly abstract. However, the essential logic of each model ties its elements together. Research has shown that decisions may be made primarily on the basis of objective reason, consensus, routine or custom, relative power, coincidence, or some combination of these factors. Researchers have held up the models as templates through which they view the actual decision process, matching behavior with elements on the template. Only by having a number of elements in each theory and by stating them abstractly has this identification been possible.

By following an analogous process, administrators can also benefit from post facto analysis of decisions in their organizations. They can consider past decisions that worked out well and those that didn't, determining the extent to which it was the process itself that accounted for success or failure. It is a rare administrator who has never seen a well-conceived decision result in unpleasant surprises, often because critical elements of the process were obscured, misunderstood, or forgotten. By applying the models to past and current decisions, administrators can develop insights about what process can achieve desired results. Rather than merely saying, "We must be doing something right," an administrator can pinpoint that "something." Conversely, if something is wrong, an administrator can identify and correct the factors that contribute to the problem. The chief advantage of using models to analyze events is that they create distance between decisionmakers and decisions. Administrators can step back from a particular situation and ask,"What is going on here? What process are we actually using? and What assumptions are guiding this process?"

A remark that a vice-president for finance once made to me may reflect the sentiments of many administrators: "I know perfectly well how to make rational decisions. What I need to know is how to win political support for them." This remark seems to imply that his own cognitive processes are rational while the setting in which he exercises them is not. The error here is confusion of individual and organizational processes. In order to exert control over the decision process, administrators must recognize this process as an organizational phenomenon and structure it accordingly. In most organizational decisions, and certainly in the most important ones, it is not enough for one person to approach the task rationally. Since many people and groups are involved in making the decision, it is the pattern of their interactions that will determine whether the process and its outcome are rational or not.

Having dealt with the major concerns administrators express regarding the usefulness of models, we turn our attention to the five models most often associated with higher-education decisions. Before examining the differences between them, we will see what similarities there are, focusing particularly on choice, process, and change.

The Decision Process

The process of making a decision involves *choice*, *process*, and *change*. Although the need to make a decision may arise from forces that are beyond administrative control, the decision itself is, by definition, controllable. The organization has a *choice* among many alternative courses of action. For instance, a college's income from investments may have drastically declined because of a recession. This is a circumstance over which an administrator has no control. But the college's response to the situation is a choice its administrators make: does it "choose" to change its investments? Or to increase its other revenues? Or to cut its expenditures? And by what process does it make that choice?

Process is used quite deliberately to emphasize that decision-making is active—it involves interactions among people, and it requires time to unfold. It begins with the apparent need for a decision and continues through the decision itself to its effect on the organization. Moreover, the results of the choice and consequent feedback become part of the process, producing either reinforcement or modification of the decision.

The idea of results brings us to the third category that all organizational decisions have in common: *change*. The result of an organizational decision is a change in the organization. For instance, a comprehensive college that is losing students may decide, on the basis of a market survey, to add a program in computer technology. But when that decision is implemented, the result is a change in the organization: reassigned faculty must prepare new courses and new faculty may be hired; new demands on computer hardware must be accommodated through new equipment or cooperative arrangements; the admissions office may need to modify its recruiting plans.

Figure 1 depicts common features of the organizational decisionmaking process. According to this diagram, choice has three underlying features and three consequences. Underlying features are:

1. The values of the organization and the actors within it
2. The alternative courses of action considered
3. The premise directing the consideration of alternatives

Ellen Earle Chaffee

Consequences are:

1. An implementation procedure for carrying out the choice
2. Results consisting of changes both external and internal
3. Feedback that acts as both output and input

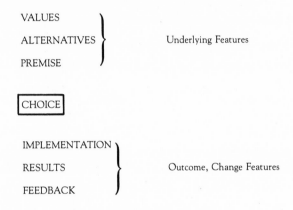

VALUES

ALTERNATIVES   Underlying Features

PREMISE

CHOICE

IMPLEMENTATION

RESULTS   Outcome, Change Features

FEEDBACK

FIGURE 1.

Elements of Choice

How might the organizational decision process work for a decision involving higher education? The decision by the University of California, announced in *The Chronicle of Higher Education*, June 30, 1982, to increase from 11 to 16 the number of yearlong, basic high-school courses required for entrance to the university provides a good example for study.

1. Judging from the discussion that preceded this decision, we may surmise that the *values* guiding it were largely academic: the university wanted to upgrade the academic preparation of its entering students to permit more advanced undergraduate coursework.

2. *Alternatives* for accomplishing this objective were many: inferior students could be eliminated through a required

course; graduation requirements could be stiffened; special summer sessions could be offered to underprepared freshmen. 3. Guiding this choice was the *premise* that students who had taken 16 courses would perform better than students who had taken 11.

Consequences of the *choice* could mean substantial changes:

1. *Implementation* would involve changing not just UC's admissions practices, but the entire high-school curriculum for the state.
2. *Results* would be felt throughout the state and the university.
3. These results would be evaluated on the basis of *feedback* from student outcomes and other studies. If the new entrance requirements were perceived as beneficial, in fact promoting the values that initially motivated the decision, they would be retained or even augmented. If not, they would be lowered or other courses of action might be initiated.

Theoretically, this is how the decision process works.

The Rational Model

What has been described in the foregoing example is the rational model of decisionmaking. Because a greater value has been placed on order and logic than on chaos and intuition in Western culture, much has been written about this model. The rational approach is inherent in the economic theory of the firm, in the scientific method, and in such prepackaged management tools as Planning-Programming-Budgeting Systems and Management by Objectives. Table 1 presents the features of a generic rational model. (Features enclosed in rectangular boxes will be explained in chapter 2 as elements of the model that can be empirically tested.)

Ellen Earle Chaffee

TABLE 1

The Rational Model:
Deciding by Reasoned Problem Solving

Decision Element	Characteristics	Implications
VALUES	Known, a priori * Single preference list Consistent with goal	Superordinate goal
ALTERNATIVES	Means to desired ends *	Search for possible solutions
PREMISE	Maximize	Simultaneous consideration of alternatives * Central arena for deliberation Causal relations understood
CHOICE	Select maximizing * alternative	Active, conscious choice
IMPLEMENTATION	Enact details of choice	Unified support
RESULTS	Intended consequences	Causal relations understood
FEEDBACK	Information useful for understanding causal relations, nature of the problem	Capacity to use such information—analytic skill, open mindedness, input procedures

Success in using this model within a continuing organization requires:
Unity of and commitment to purpose or goal
A production technology that can be understood
Sequential rather than concurrent or reversed timing through the process

*Boxed items are the basis for testing Stanford's budget process, reported in Chapter 2.

Values

The first feature, values, is a major source of controversy because of its underlying premise that decisionmakers possess known values, ordered according to relative preferences, prior to making decisions. The issues arising in discussion of this feature are (1) whether it is possible for an individual, much less a collection of individuals, to rank a set of diverse values into a single preference list, and (2) whether values are not actually identified *after* decisionmakers have made up their minds on some other grounds. For instance, college entrance requirements were relaxed in the '60s largely because of political pressure to admit greater proportions of disadvantaged and minority students. After that political decision had been made, many administrators discovered that providing equal opportunities to students of all backgrounds was indeed a worthy goal. But the initial decision could not be considered truly rational unless evidence were produced showing that the college had in fact considered equal opportunity important *before* it took actions to improve access.

However, the a priori values requirement does make at least conceptual sense if it is viewed in the context of one or more superordinate goals, such as service to constituents or academic excellence, that act as an organizing principle, a focus of committed action. The goal must be stable and must have real meaning for the participants. With such goals, participants can at least agree about why they are involved, although their recommended courses of action may vary. If the value structure of the actors is known prior to their considering alternatives and making a choice, and if the values are consistent with a larger goal of the organization, the process will exhibit at least some of the requisite characteristics of an ordered list of preferences. When the preferences reflect commonly understood interests of the college, commitment of the college president only, because he or she is a key decisionmaker, is sufficient to substantiate the claim that a college had a prior value premise.

Alternatives

The rational model's alternative courses of action constitute means to the ends implied by the values. The premise underlying choice is then to maximize the likelihood of achieving those ends. To make the comparisons implied by this kind of choice, actors must consider the array of alternatives simultaneously. They must have some central arena or forum in which to place and examine the alternatives, and they must understand the processes by which cause-and-effect relationships turn inputs into outputs (production functions). That is, they must have some grounds for believing that engaging in a chosen activity will produce the expected results.

Choice

In this model, choice is a deliberate action. When, how, and by whom the decision is made should be identifiable. At the time of decision, participants are theoretically capable of predicting the results or probable results of choice, and those outcomes are foreseen and intended.

Implementation, Results, and Feedback

In the rational model, implementation is straightforward; the list of preferences and the logic behind the decision should lessen dissent and surprise. The results are organizational changes that, as we saw in the case of the California decision, may go far beyond the organization and may produce feedback. The users of feedback information must have the analytical skills to understand it, the openmindedness to be receptive to it, and the orderly procedures to channel it back into the decision process.

Several conditions are necessary for an organization to use the rational model successfully. The actors must share a common goal or set of goals, and they must have reasonably congruent ideas and attitudes about how to achieve them. They must be engaged in processes for which they understand cause-effect relationships. To the extent that the problem is complex, they need technical competence to unravel those relationships. Finally, they must enact the process sequentially, as presented in table 1, with respect to each problem, which requires time and patience.

Rational decisionmaking does not necessarily produce superior decisions. But even if it did, organizational dynamics are so complex that the sole use of the rational model over time might blind decisionmakers to important phenomena, thus narrowing interactions and thought processes in ways that would eventually become counterproductive. Schools that bowed to political pressure in the '60s may have made some refreshing discoveries about students and curricula that became part of these schools' permanent values, providing new input that could then be absorbed through use of the rational model.

One great advantage of the rational model is that the rational decisionmaking process can be a unifying one, binding the actors together rather than dividing them. This unifying property also characterizes the next model we shall examine, the collegial.

The Collegial Model

It has been traditionally assumed that colleges and universities make most of their decisions according to a model named for these institutions: the collegial model. According to this view, institutions are directed by the faculty, acting as peers who reason together toward their common goals. This is indeed an idyllic picture, but is it accurate? The consensus among today's higher-education managers is that while the collegial model may apply to academic decisions, it does not describe the non-academic decisions that cause the greatest problems for administrators.

As shown in table 2, the collegial decision rests on the value of shared responsibility. When a new faculty member is to be hired, for instance, other members are expected to contribute to decisionmaking by looking closely at vitas, discussing strengths and weaknesses of each candidate vis-à-vis the needs of the department, and minimizing their personal preferences in the interest of upgrading the department through the selection of the best possible candidate. When the decision is made, moreover, it must satisfy all participants sufficiently to produce commitment to the choice: if no candidate meets the participants' criteria, none is selected, and the search process continues. In fact, most departments function well as hiring committees, and the decision to hire could not be as competently made by any other method.

Academic decisions about required courses, required reading lists, and requisites of all kinds lend themselves to use of the collegial model, though interdepartmental decisions about these matters may become political. To the question, What courses shall be required for a humanistic education? faculty in most departments will answer that their subjects are requisite, and rightly so. The classicist, the philosopher, the mathematician whose life has been devoted to a professional field is expressing not just self-interest but sincere belief in the importance of that field by fighting for its survival.

It should not be supposed that professors are more capable than others of making a collegial decision. Indeed, their independence of mind and ability to verbalize ideas emphasize differences that less active minds might be willing to overlook. In a college I visited recently, the Department of Humanities was so

TABLE 2

The Collegial Model:
Deciding by Consensus

Decision Element	Characteristics	Implications
VALUES	Shared responsibility	Actors share fundamental premises about organizational purpose and process Equal opportunity to contribute to decision
ALTERNATIVES	Determined by backgrounds and interests of participants and by interplay in discussion	Iterative and interactive development of alternatives; wide range of alternatives likely
PREMISE	Consensus	Participants are willing to explain, defend, receive new information and ideas, change their minds, take time to meet and discuss
CHOICE	Agree on a solution that satisfies most or all	Willing to compromise for the general welfare
IMPLEMENTATION	Delegated or enacted by each person affected	Widespread commitment to the choice is assumed
RESULTS	Organic change	In decisions involving major change, transitions are likely to be relatively smooth
FEEDBACK	Informal, ad hoc	Depends on participants' observations and priorities

Success in using this model within a continuing organization requires:
Consensus on fundamental premises
Time and opportunity for discussion
Participants with open minds, mutual respect

fragmented that its members were not only incapable of having a meeting but even of agreeing on the wording of the agenda for the meeting. And even in departments that seem harmonious, decisions about such matters as the assignment of teaching loads create dissension not easily solved in a collegial manner.

Ellen Earle Chaffee

One application of the collegial model that administrators often do not adequately explore is decisions that affect staff. In a time of scarcity, for instance, when cutbacks are necessary and are understood to be necessary, many staff employees would be willing to work together to effect savings rather than have jobs eliminated. Staff members frequently understand the workings of a college or university better than faculty members, are more willing to accept change in order to keep the institution running smoothly, and could provide valuable input to the decision-making process if their potential were realized.

The Political Model

Reference has been made to the political model as a typical, sometimes appropriate approach for interdepartmental decisions. Some students of decision theory contend that all decisions made by a university are political. The university, these critics maintain, is not like a corporation (the rational model) but is much more like a political entity in its pluralism and in its recognition of the legitimacy of internal conflict.

Conflict resolution is the basis of the political model, as shown in table 3. Theorists assume that organizational actors have multiple conflicting values and objectives that are determined primarily by their self-interests. Actors in an organization, whether individuals or subunits such as academic departments, presumably are knit together by some mutually understood purpose. However, proponents of the political model argue that this general purpose does not constitute a goal embodying the actors' partisan self-interests. Rather it provides a forum (the organization) in which actors work out the differences among themselves. The differences exist because actors intend for the final decision to favor them or their departments in preference to others. When an opportunity to choose arises, the position of each actor is determined by the actor's stake in the results.

TABLE 3

The Political Model:
Deciding through Conflict Resolution

Decision Element	Characteristics	Implications
VALUES	Multiple, nonconsensual, based on self-interest	Actors have varying interests apart from any superordinate goal
ALTERNATIVES	Expressions of actors' self-interests	Partisan—determined by stakes, attention Proposed by actors
PREMISE	Win	Survival of fittest force Coalition building Arena for negotiation
CHOICE	Ratify the proposal of the prevailing bloc	Probably unintended by any single actor Little or no causal link between objectives and results
IMPLEMENTATION	Certify and monitor details of choice	Tinkering with details
RESULTS	Negotiated consequences of choice	Changes in organizational conditions
FEEDBACK	Relative changes in actor strength and organizational conditions	

Success in using this model within a continuing organization requires:
  Diversity of interests among actors
  Representation of organization's interests in composite of actors' interests
  Power fairly evenly distributed
  Availability of arenas for negotiation and for choice ratification

If only one actor's welfare is at stake, no conflict exists and the political model is not activated. If only two actors are involved, presumably the issue will be decided by one overpowering the other. On occasion, however, the less powerful actor is able to withdraw some critical resource in retaliation. When two actors are thus deadlocked, or when more actors have stakes in the decision, the process of the political model begins. It is worked out interactively among the actors, through negotiation or bargaining and coalition building.

An example of this process occurred at a midwestern campus in the spring of 1982 when the dean of arts and sciences was forced by a vice-chancellor (the more powerful actor) to accept budget cuts and retaliated by withdrawing a critical resource—25 sections of expository writing, required for graduation by most of the professional schools. The dean also cut the English department's budget, and that department in turn retaliated by withdrawing classes in technical writing, again a required course for some schools.

It is not difficult to see how far these actions deviate from the rational and collegial models of decisionmaking. Obviously, a strong central administration guided by a priori values and presented with an array of alternatives would not choose to eliminate courses required by students for graduation. Nor would a group of professors motivated by desire to arrive at a consensus that expressed their common preferences make such choices. The actions were frankly partisan and, in the eyes of their promulgators, completely justified as the only methods of self-defense against stronger forces.

Whether or not justified, however, the choices made illustrate the deficiencies of the political model as a basis for guiding a university. The major drawback is that this approach makes no provision for a superordinate goal. The educational function of the university is not simply "forgotten" in the midst of the power struggle; it has only a rhetorical place in the struggle. The second drawback is that the result of the struggle cannot be predicted—results cannot be causally linked to objectives—and the final consequence may not serve the interests of any parties. Since neither the English department nor the College of Arts and Sciences was awarded more funds, the only results of political action were that students were deprived of courses they needed and wanted, and that considerable disruption occurred.

FIVE MODELS OF ORG. DECISIONMAKING

Some theorists argue that such disruption is healthy for an organization, drawing attention to critical interests that otherwise might be abridged or go unrecognized. They also point out that the political model is more efficient than a model requiring consensus: action can be taken despite differences. Finally, they contend that if all of the interests of the organization are represented, if power is distributed evenly enough to promote coalitions, and if an arena is provided where bargaining can occur, political decisionmaking can bring creative solutions that have widespread acceptance.

Most theorists who see the university as a political structure do not advocate that structure, however; they simply see universities as political organizations incapable of rational decisions. Though universities must deal with complex issues, they have poorly defined strategies, relatively autonomous actors, and little consensus about goals and priorities. The budgeting process in particular is cited as a political activity in which "the rich get richer": successful use of power brings benefits that add power for use in the next round. And finally, a fundamental conflict may exist between faculty values and the needs of a rational administration: according to a 1979 study by Poulton, faculty are inherently unsympathetic toward such administrative priorities as long-range planning, facility in quantitative thought, and skill in management techniques. As chapter 2 will show, however, all of these difficulties can be overcome by an administrator who is sufficiently dedicated to the rational process.

The Bureaucratic Model

While the political model may provide highly visible decision situations, in higher-education institutions, as in all organizations, most decisions are reached by a process so unobtrusive that it has rarely been explored by theorists: the bureaucratic

Ellen Earle Chaffee

model. As noted in table 4, both the characteristics and implications of this model are so narrowly focused that the actors in the decision may not even be aware that they are making a decision.

TABLE 4

The Bureaucratic Model:
Deciding by Structured Interaction Patterns

Decision Element	Characteristics	Implications
VALUES	Operational efficiency	Hierarchical organization
ALTERNATIVES	Historical No search outside routine	Limited repertoire Tradition-oriented Organization-centered
PREMISE	It worked before	Predictability of results
CHOICE	Identify the output of the procedure	Procedure is more interesting than substance of an issue Focus on procedure activa- tion more than on decision
IMPLEMENTATION	Determined by sub- routines	
RESULTS	Predictable from organization's structure and rules of interaction	Organization is very slow to change
FEEDBACK	Repetition	Marginal adaptations of routines and routine- activation processes

Success in using this model within a continuing organization requires:
    Standard operating routines useful for current demands
    Marginal adaptations of routines and routine-activation procedures
    Workable system for triggering appropriate routines

In 1971, Allison described this model as "the organizational process," in which the organization's hierarchical structure and systematized routines, or standard operating procedures, are the major determinants of the decision process. The underlying rationale for the model is efficiency: systematic procedures can be used to institutionalize what an organization has learned over time. Because of this orderliness and orientation toward efficiency, some authors do not distinguish between the rational and bureaucratic models—they may use either term to refer to either model as described here. I separate the two, as does Allison, because the models tend to deal with two fundamentally different kinds of decisions. The rational model is well-suited to problems that are complex, nonrecurring, and novel to the organization, because it allows for treating each situation as unique and it can accommodate fresh intuitions and perceptions. The bureaucratic model, on the other hand, is most effective when applied to routine, often relatively unimportant situations. Thus, one might try a rational process for estimating the financial impact of a new government regulation and deciding how to respond to it, but use bureaucratic procedures to decide what brand of photocopier to buy.

University budgeting is apt to be more influenced by the bureaucratic than by any other model, because last year's budget base usually determines over 90 percent of this year's budget. In the interests of operational efficiency within a hierarchical organization, historical alternatives alone are considered unless there is some reason to search outside the prescribed routine. Zero-based budgeting, for instance, can rarely be considered without generating great uncertainty and discontinuity, causing organizational chaos. The alternatives are thus tied to the organization and to traditional patterns, with a limited repertoire of choices. The underlying premise, "It worked before," yields predictable if unimaginative results, and the choice is replication of past decisions. The procedure is more important to participants than the substance of the decision: each actor jealously guards both the budget base and the right to be part of the budgeting process even when there is little possibility of change.

Ellen Earle Chaffee

Implementation of bureaucratic decisionmaking as seen in budgeting consists mainly of incrementalism or decrementalism. In times of plenty, incrementalism is usually automatic; in times of scarcity, however, decrementalism does not become similarly automatic. Studies have shown that the bureaucratic model may be inadequate in times of scarcity, and the political model tends to determine which budgets are cut more or less than others. In contrast with the model presented in table 4, the result is a sudden shift from predictability to change.

It was precisely to avoid sudden shifts from the bureaucratic to the political model that the rational model for the budgeting process was developed at Stanford. Placed within the framework of universitywide goals, the budgeting procedure provided its own feedback for self-evaluation and permitted a middle ground between stasis and disruption.

Neither the bureaucratic nor the political model, however, is capable of producing shifts in direction as sudden as those caused by the model that was christened "organized anarchy" by Cohen and March in 1974.

Organized Anarchy

This final category of decisionmaking, as depicted in table 5, takes place through accidents of timing and interest. In their study of university leadership, Cohen and March identified common characteristics promoting this type of decisionmaking as diversity of goals, ill-understood technology, and scarcity of time and resources. The ambiguity created by these characteristics made purposeful forms of action impossible. Seeing the university as an organized anarchy, the authors described choice in this circumstance as a garbage can in which all sorts of problems, solutions, and participants mix.

FIVE MODELS OF ORG. DECISIONMAKING

TABLE 5

Organized Anarchy: Deciding by Accident

Decision Element	Characteristics	Implications
VALUES	Diffuse, multiple Triggered by choice opportunity	Significance of attention Fluid participation
ALTERNATIVES	Floating problems and solutions	Ambiguity of intention
PREMISE	Accident	Complexity, ambiguity Causal relations unknown Unknown technology
CHOICE	Ratify coincidence	Non-purposeful
IMPLEMENTATION	Incidental	
RESULTS	Incidental	Erroneous "lessons of the past"
FEEDBACK	New problems, solutions, actors	

Success in using this model within a continuing organization requires:
   Sensible foolishness

The values of actors are diffuse and multiple; they come into play only when an actor perceives an opportunity for choice. One determinant of the outcome of a choice, then, is which actors make their presences and concerns known in the decision process. Their current problems or solutions then become the alternatives. Any sense of purpose about the choice is bound to be illusory under these conditions, a phenomenon that the authors term "ambiguity of intention."

The logic of this model is that of a traffic collision. Since the technology whereby the organization produces outcomes is not understood, cause-effect relationships are unknown and therefore cannot direct the matching of problems with solutions. Just as the logic behind Mr. Jones and Ms. Smith driving at 30 mph into an intersection at right angles to one another is obscure, so is the logic of organized anarchy. Indeed, Cohen and March liken the university president in this situation to the driver of a skidding automobile. The choice action is a kind of ratification of coincidence that is not purposeful in the sense of linking objectives with intended results.

Implementation and results follow in a similarly confused way, presumably, and create new problems, solutions, and motivated actors for another round. Choice events do not in fact show the actors which causes produce which results, but because they may appear to do so, actors learn erroneous lessons from the past. Cohen and March provide the only possible perspective from which to view the response of decisionmakers in an organization that acts in this way—they call it "sensible foolishness." They suggest a need for playfulness and offer a number of guidelines for actors.

Undoubtedly, readers can supply examples of this apparently random process from their own experiences. A recurring example, particularly among small colleges, is the search for a new president or a new head of a powerful department. The search committee, armed with erroneous "lessons of the past," is determined to choose a new administrator who will not have the faults of the present one. Individual members inject diffuse, multiple values triggered by the choice opportunity rather than by a prior standard for judging a potential administrator in terms of the college's continuing goals and needs. They envision alternatives mainly in terms of current problems; how these problems arose and, more importantly, how other problems were avoided are unknown to them. If they happen to select a satisfactory candidate, the choice is due more to accident than design. Indeed, while a search committee must be conscientious and intelligent while engaging in its tremendously important task, its members might also realize that they are in a situation that calls for "sensible foolishness"; that is, no choice is going to be perfect, and they may as well expect a round of new problems.

This fact became clear to me when I visited a small Eastern college in connection with a research project on strategic recovery from financial difficulty. The college had recently replaced its president, a coldly efficient administrator who had antagonized faculty and students, with a charming, warm humanitarian who passionately believed in collegial decisionmaking. Indeed, he had alienated several potential donors by refusing to tell them what future direction the college would take on grounds that this must be a group decision. I found him an enchanting conversationalist, but, in an hour's interview, I was unable to ferret out a single issue or statistic relating to the college's budget. Not only was he unaware that external constituencies were essential to the college's financial health, but he seemed to find the whole subject of finances mysterious and somewhat distasteful. When I expressed surprise at this attitude in a later conversation with the bursar, that gentleman sighed and shook his head. "He's a bright, wonderful guy—exactly what we thought we wanted," he said, "but his attitude toward money is putting us out of business."

Sharing his obvious concern, I asked, "How do you sleep at night?"

"Like a baby," he said with a weak smile. "I sleep for an hour, wake up and cry, sleep for another hour, and that goes on all night."

This anecdote illustrates not only the hazards of organized anarchy but also the paradox that colleges and universities, despite their vast reserves of brainpower, are not noted for skill in managing their own affairs. A major reason for this deficiency, I believe, is that college and university administrators tend to devote their attention to a problem situation and its solutions— the *substance* of a decision—and to forget that achieving a satisfactory outcome may depend heavily on the *process* by which they reach a decision. This chapter has attempted to show that the decision process within an organization is extremely complex and that decision theory suggests five ways of structuring this process, which differ widely in characteristics, implications, and applications. Four of these—the collegial, political, bureaucratic, and anarchic—have been empirically studied with regard to higher education; the fifth—the rational—has hardly been acknowledged in empirical studies. Chapter 2 will therefore present an in-depth study of the rational model as exemplified by the budgeting process at Stanford during the 1970s.

A Case Study of the Rational Model

A major problem with decision theory is that its links with reality are seldom tested. Rational decisionmaking in particular is generally conceded to be a normative ideal not susceptible to practice. It is thought to be unrealistic, because rational theory prescribes an ordered sequence of events that cannot be followed in real decisions and because it requires powers of search and comprehension beyond human capability for most decision problems of typical complexity.

The tendency in higher-education literature has been to identify institutional decision processes with the political, collegial, or organized-anarchy models. The bureaucratic model is assumed but considered unimportant, while the rational model has been considered so stringent in its theoretical demands that only a few previous studies have made even a partial effort to test for it in higher education.

In this chapter I will discuss previous studies very briefly, present a test for the rational model, compare the results of my study of budgeting practices at Stanford University over a ten-year period with the test criteria, and draw a conclusion about the feasibility of the rational model.

Ellen Earle Chaffee

Conclusions from Previous Studies

I chose to focus on budgeting for three reasons. First, a budget is a program plan in monetary terms that both determines and expresses an organization's goals through its activities. Therefore, it seems an appropriate vehicle through which to test for the goal-oriented, rational approach. Second, it produces measurable decisions and reliable records that can be used to place each year's budget decision in historical perspective. And third, unlike other areas of decisionmaking in which there is virtually no precedent for empirical studies of this kind, three previous studies were available that documented budgeting practices at three universities.

In the first study of its kind, Pfeffer and Salancik (1974) used data from the University of Illinois over a thirteen-year period to identify what criteria are used in making budget decisions and, more particularly, whether a power criterion associated with the political model is a significant predictor. They found both the bureaucratic and political models significant; other factors such as department size, cost per student, national rank, and membership of the department in a particular college did not provide satisfactory explanations of budgets. They did not conduct tests for the rational or collegial models.

In 1978, Hills and Mahoney used a modified version of the Illinois method to analyze data from the University of Minnesota, but with a significant addition: they divided the data into two sets of years—abundant resources versus scarce resources—and weighted the effects of incrementalism and political power for each set. Not surprisingly, they found that incrementalism was more apparent during abundance than during scarcity, and that in abundant years, decisionmakers made attempts not evident during years of scarcity to equate budgets with workloads among departments. In times of scarcity, moreover, the political model was more evident than it was in times of abundance.

A third study, published by Pfeffer and Moore in 1980 and related to two campuses of the University of California, again focused on the bureaucratic and political models. Their findings essentially agreed with those of the other two studies: budgeting was bureaucratic and political, with the latter approach more apparent on the campus with scarcer resources.

Like the Illinois study, neither the Minnesota nor the California study tested for the rational model as I have defined it here. These studies treated the terms *bureaucratic* and *rational* as if they were synonymous but dealt with variables that were bureaucratic.

History of the Budget Process at Stanford

My study of the Stanford budget process focused on the ten-year period from 1970 through 1979 and covered allocation of general funds to the 38 academic departments within the university that existed throughout the period of study. Nonacademic departments were excluded because their budget issues were different and were decided by a different process.

Some history of administrative policy at Stanford is helpful in understanding the significance of the budget process there. Fred Terman, the provost when Stanford was emerging as a leading research university, was described by a colleague as "a one-man everything" who knew more about the academic units at Stanford than those inside them knew. Deans who met with him to present their budget requests had to be well prepared to face his acute and penetrating questions. After his retirement in 1965, the university spent six years in a turmoil of student unrest and changing leadership. The budget process, like other administrative functions, necessarily took a back seat to more urgent matters and was fragmented by a succession of leaders.

When William F. Miller became provost in 1971, he appointed Raymond F. Bacchetti as vice-provost for budget and planning and changed the process for allocating resources from the so-called poker model, with one dealer and a host of players, to a systems model with a detailed procedure. In an interview I conducted with Bacchetti on July 22, 1980, he described this procedure as "the mortal representation of the Olympian Terman, who by dint of his authority and knowledge, got the deans to behave as the protocol now specifies."

In developing this system, Miller and Bacchetti were motivated not only by financial interests but also by the desire to set up a procedure that would result in decisions that were related to the university's major program goals, planned in accordance with such goals, and evaluated on the basis of those goals—that is, rational decisions. How well did they succeed? In order to answer that question, I stated five criteria that I considered essential to the rational approach and then compared the budget events during the decade with these criteria.

Criteria to Test for the Rational Model

The five criteria selected for application to the budget process were restatements of the items in boxes in table 1:

1. *Values and Objectives*: a preexisting set of values and objectives for budgeting should be formulated in accordance with the values and objectives of the university as a whole.
2. *Alternatives*: a set of alternative courses of action, means to the ends described by the objectives, should be arrayed for simultaneous consideration; in budgeting, these alternatives are requests for funds.

A CASE STUDY OF THE RATIONAL MODEL

3. *Centralization of Decisionmaking*: the structure of the decision process should assure that a central authority makes final budget decisions.

4. *Understanding of Consequences*: each request should be accompanied by analysis of its costs, benefits, and other consequences.

5. *Value-maximizing Choice*: the choices made should in fact advance the values and objectives chosen for the budget process. Quantitative data should document the correspondence between objectives and results.

Application to the Budget Process

Values and Objectives

Miller's administration had two major objectives in its allocation of resources throughout the 1970s, each clearly stated in available correspondence. The first was to achieve budget equilibrium in which growth rates of income and expense were in balance. The second was to allocate funds on the basis of well-defined academic criteria.

Equilibrium. The decade began with a Budget Adjustment Program (BAP) to close what was seen as a $6 million gap between income and expense by 1975 and to equalize rates of increase for income and expense. These targets, which constituted a macro-level budget objective for the university as a whole, set the financial parameters for budgeting in the early 1970s.

The BAP program was succeeded by a three-year Budget Equilibrium Program (BEP), designed to cut expenses and improve income by $10 million and also to achieve equilibrium by 1979-1980. Estimates for annual targets were made on the basis of the Long Range Financial Forecast (LRFF), which relied on advanced methods and equipment for gathering and analyzing information.

33

Ellen Earle Chaffee

Incorporated into each year's budget discussions was consideration of the specific reductions or "gap-closing measures" each school or unit head planned to make in order to help achieve the overall goals. Letters documenting these discussions between the provost and the deans show that Miller was as interested in knowing the priorities and procedures the deans used to identify economies as he was in knowing specifically what the gap-closing measures would be.

Academic Objectives. Given limited resources, the provost's criteria for funding programs were:

1. Academic importance
2. Student interest
3. Possibility for excellence in the program
4. Funding potential

I will explain what these phrases meant to Miller later in this section. Stanford records show that these four criteria were often and clearly stated from 1972 through 1980; they formed the backbone of Miller's selective budgeting intentions throughout the decade.

However, the identification of consistent criteria is not enough to confirm the presence of the rational model. For instance, if the criteria were set by, or favored, a coalition, the process might be political. If they could be plugged into a computer to produce budget decisions by some consistent algorithm, the model might be bureaucratic. If they represented a value system for which there was consensus in the organization, the collegial model could not be ruled out.

Determining academic importance, for instance, would seem to be a collegial decision, since the provost could not be expected to have expertise in every field. However, as a detailed description of the budget procedure will show, the decision to fund a program did not depend on the will of a group, as the collegial model specifies. While each dean consulted individually with department leaders before asking the provost for funds, no group discussion of school budget needs occurred.

The second criterion, student interest, has been most consistently related to the bureaucratic and political models in previous studies. The number of instructional units taught is readily measured and easily translated into dollars for budgeting. If a university allocates funds in proportion to amount of teaching, the bureaucratic model may be present. If the size of a department determines its power in the system, and larger departments get disproportionately more general funds, the political model is a possibility.

At Stanford, the correlation between instructional units taught and general funds budgeted for 38 departments over 10 years was .82, indicating a strong relationship between teaching and budgeting. However, close analysis showed that the relationship was strongest in the departments that did relatively little or average amounts of teaching. The correlation for the smallest 75 percent of the departments was .87, while that for the 25 percent of departments doing the most teaching was an insignificant .01. Thus, since the largest departments did not receive funds in proportion to student credit hours, the budgeting process on the basis of student interest seemed neither bureaucratic nor political.

The third criterion, the possibility for academic excellence, is clearly central to the mission of a leading research university wishing to maintain its position. The goal of excellence was the foundation of Terman's approach, bringing Stanford into national prominence and giving rise to the metaphor "steeples of excellence" to describe the aspirations of the university. "Excellence" is more fully explained in section 5, and in a research report (Chaffee 1982).

Finally, Miller defined the fourth criterion, funding potential, in terms of both security and adequacy of funds. He applied this criterion more often when closing or creating a department than when differentiating among continuing departments. For example, in a 1975 letter to the dean of engineering explaining his decision to close the program in architecture, he cited lack of support from nongeneral funds sources as a threat to both security and adequacy.

Thus all four academic criteria were rationally oriented as well as consistently reaffirmed throughout the decade.

Alternatives

Second, in a rational process, the provost would simultaneously consider a wide array of spending alternatives every year. The key terms to be tested are "simultaneously" and "wide array." The test is simplified since the chronology of budgeting events each year, based on traditions that extend back to the 1950s at Stanford, remained essentially the same throughout Miller's term of office. Also, the chronology was devised in accordance with the goal he stated in a letter to the deans, May 10, 1972, in which he called for a "regular budget process during which all budget requests are laid out together for simultaneous review—that is, we will not make piecemeal decisions about the Budget. . . ." The chronology, presented as appendix A, covered a period of 18 months—April through the following November —and set aside different blocks of time for consideration of the "equilibrium" objective and the "academic criteria" objective.

Equilibrium. Obviously, the basis for all budgeting is a clear picture of available funds, and Stanford used its technical expertise to make that picture as accurate as possible. Both the Long Range Financial Forecast (LRFF) and a one-year set of analyses called Parameters Papers were used to assess rates of increase in projected income and expense. The LRFF, a computerized model that began with the actual budget of the current year and extrapolated projected budgets for the next five years, served as the basis for the more detailed Parameters Papers. Extrapolations were made using estimates of the Consumer Price Index, expected increases in costs such as energy supplies, and other assumptions coming from wherever expertise was likely to be found—on campus from faculty economists and computer scientists, or from such people as physical-plant managers; off campus from analyses by banks, utility companies, and others. Forecasts were run a number of times with varying assumptions to allow for all reasonable possibilities.

In addition to technical expertise, the achievement of equilibrium required constant communication. Academic and business officers involved with the budget met weekly during the forecast period and biweekly with the provost; through these meetings, the provost developed a sense of those events he could control and those he could not, gaining a perspective of the alternatives available to him.

Academic Objectives. The provost's alternatives for expenditure were drawn from the academic units according to the protocol process shown in figure 2. The provost wrote to each dean describing the constraints suggested by the LRFF and Parameters Papers and posing detailed questions about the school's plans. These constraints included the provost's estimates of across-the-board increases for salaries and other categories of expense. He then met with the deans individually to discuss their wishes and his convictions, and each dean wrote a budget letter detailing special requests for nonincremental funds. The vice-provost prepared a detailed list of all such requests, humorously called the "migration analysis" because it reflected the need for entries to "migrate" out of the funding column until the sum of the column was within equilibrium constraints. This list and the documentation provided by the deans gave the provost the opportunity to consider alternative expenditures simultaneously, in principle according to his objectives for important, excellent, securely funded programs of interest to students. Furthermore, there is evidence that the provost rejected attempts to circumvent the process by bringing requests forward at any time other than that demanded by protocol. Thus, the criterion of simultaneous alternatives was unequivocally satisfied.

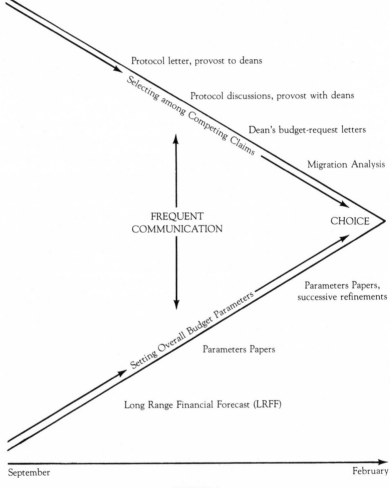

FIGURE 2.
Chronology of Events in Budget Decisions
SOURCE: Raymond F. Bacchetti, Academic Planning Office Seminar,
Stanford University, 16 October 1978.

A CASE STUDY OF THE RATIONAL MODEL

Whether the provost had a "wide" range of nonincremental alternatives to consider is a matter of judgment, but he did have many alternatives. In the seven years for which complete sets of deans' budget letters could be found, 284 requests for additional money from general funds were made on behalf of the 38 departments in the study, or 40.6 per year, with a mean of $9,255 per request and a range of $200 to $15,000. Documentation of decisions on these requests is available for the last four years of the study only. During that time, the provost had 156 requests, authorized funds for 97 of these (62 percent), but authorized full funding for only 36 (23 percent). He therefore had four times as many alternatives as he thought merited full funding: while their breadth was not measurable, their number was sufficient to constitute an "array," in accordance with the second criterion.

Centralization

Centralization was achieved through the structure of the budget process. Departments decided which requests for special increases would be forwarded for the provost's consideration; they also played an advisory role in the budget reduction programs. However, the deans had the final decision, not only about programs but also about faculty hiring, promotion, and salaries. They, rather than the department heads, were in direct communication with the provost.

Further, through chairing the biweekly budget group meetings and through close association with Vice-Provost Bacchetti and with the vice-president for business and finance, Miller was sufficiently well informed about every aspect of university finance that, in contrast to some of his predecessors, he fulfilled his position as primary officer in charge of budgeting by making the necessary decisions personally.

This strongly centralized approach may seem bureaucratic, since that model depends on the hierarchy of formal authority.

But centralization is also a hallmark of rationality. It is not centralization that makes the two models different from each other. Rather, the primary distinctions between the two models are that the rational model (1) is strongly oriented toward solving problems that are new to the organization, and (2) explicitly relies on values other than functional efficiency.

Stanford's centralized approach may also seem debatable at a time when decentralized decisionmaking is being increasingly practiced by organizations. However, a centralized approach may be rendered acceptable through broad participation of those who are most affected by the decision. Since centralization is both a controversial and a significant feature of rational decisionmaking, the next chapter explains how central authority, combined with broad participation, creates the best possible setting for strategic decisions based on the rational model.

Consequences

The fourth criterion deals with the quality of information available to the provost: was it sufficient to allow him to predict the consequences of the array of alternatives among which he was required to choose? And how did the information affect choice in the two major areas of concern?

Equilibrium. In achieving the goal of financial equilibrium, both accuracy and flexibility of information were essential in guiding the university through a period in which stability had to be reestablished without jeopardizing prestige. Computer models were particularly helpful in estimating how budget alternatives would alter the university's financial picture for 3, 5, 10, and even 25 years. Further, these models were sufficiently integrated to allow, for example, the ramifications of an increase in tuition to be traced through to its effects on enrollments and financial-aid costs.

However, in Miller's terminology, these analyses were used as "a smart instrument panel, not an automatic pilot." Humans, not computers, did the piloting, relying heavily on communication and also on creative thinking. Each summer, the academic and budget staffs studied particular aspects of the budget problem in search of creative solutions. Stanford also used a system called "Autumn Revisions," in which a few requests for funding—usually for capital projects or nonessential improvements—were neither funded nor denied but put on a priority list. Income that was especially difficult to predict was also taken out of the regular budget process. When this income became certain, items on the "wish list" were then funded. Thus, budget cutting at one stage of the process, combined with additional funding at another stage, prevented the simple incrementalism of the bureaucratic model while allowing both for innovation and for circumstances unforseeable by technological means.

Academic Objectives. As described earlier, the alternatives for academic expenditures were presented to the provost by the deans in annual letters setting forth compelling arguments in favor of funding each request. They were not, and were not expected to be, unbiased; they were, however, expected to contain objective information. The question is whether this information was sufficient to allow the provost to relate requests to his preference list through an adequate understanding of costs and effects.

Annual letters from the deans were available for the last seven years of the study period, and the 165 individual requests they contained were analyzed by means of a six-item dichotomous-choice questionnaire. Scoring involved answering yes (1) or no (0) as to whether the dean's rationale:

1. Included explicit reference to meeting some goal or objective
2. Documented the need to solve the problem or meet the goal
3. Referred to alternative means of meeting the need

4. Defined results expected if the requests were funded
5. Showed that the recommended solution had the most favorable cost-benefit ratio
6. Explicitly identified the value(s) that would be expressed by funding the request

The consistent theme of relating causes with desired effects is readily apparent in these items.

Summing the number of "yes" answers yielded a score between zero and six for each request rationale. On this basis, the mean score for the 165 requests was 3.15, with a mode of 4.0. Most scores (69 percent) were either three or four. Thus, the deans gave the provost some or most, but not all, of the information he needed when they wrote their budget letters.

While this evidence for sufficient information is not strong, it is more convincing when viewed in context. The letters were, after all, only part of the communication process between deans and provost—there were personal meetings as well, which undoubtedly provided more information. Also, since the writing and reasoning styles of the deans were idiosyncratic, the letters did not lend themselves naturally to systematic analysis. Therefore, the fact that the deans' letters contained as much classifiable information as they did suggests that the provost was in a good position to choose rationally among the requests they contained.

Choice

Finally, with reasonable confirmation of the first four criteria, we must ask the crucial question: were the provost's choices consistent with his preference list? Having set up the machinery to make rational decisions about the budget, did he in fact make such decisions?

A CASE STUDY OF THE RATIONAL MODEL

Equilibrium. Success in attaining equilibrium is difficult to measure with precision because the goal was not to reduce the actual size of the budget, but to balance it in a way that tended to equate growth rates of income and expense. To this end, a $300 million Campaign for Stanford was successfully completed during the middle of the decade, allowing increased expenditures with continued excellence while avoiding tuition increases even higher than those finally decided on. There was a point beyond which, according to both human judgment and the LRFF, such increases would have been self-defeating in the long run.

Regarding the 38 departments included in the study, academic functions were explicitly identified as the heart of the university, and the faculty was recognized as the basis of those functions. Therefore, the provost chose not to economize on increases in faculty salary, which constituted 82 percent of department budgets, and these increases were pegged at one or two points above the Consumer Price Index. As could be expected, departmental budgets increased by about the same amount as the CPI during the 10 years of the study (see figure 3). However, a significant feature of the increase, as shown by the graph, is that it undergoes less severe gyrations than the CPI. More importantly, departmental increases stayed within the targeted growth rates of the LRFF, indicating that information was being used to achieve the desired cause-effect relationship between budget goals and budget decisions.

Academic Objectives. Regarding the relationship between decisions and attainment of academic objectives, the statistical methods used to measure this relationship and the resulting evidence are presented as appendix B. For those readers who do not wish to pursue this evidence in detail, a very general discussion is presented here.

Of the four objectives—academic importance, student interest, academic excellence, and funding potential—neither academic

Ellen Earle Chaffee

Stanford Budget Year	CPI Year	Stanford Increase	CPI Increase
1970-1971	1970	.06906	.05920
1971-1972	1971	.05465	.04299
1972-1973	1972	.06826	.03298
1973-1974	1973	.08811	.06625
1974-1975	1974	.06831	.10969
1975-1976	1975	.07727	.09140
1976-1977	1976	.08285	.05769
1977-1978	1977	.07553	.06452
1978-1979	1978	.08418	.07658
1979-1980	1979	.09377	.09570
Average Annual Increase:		.07620	.06970

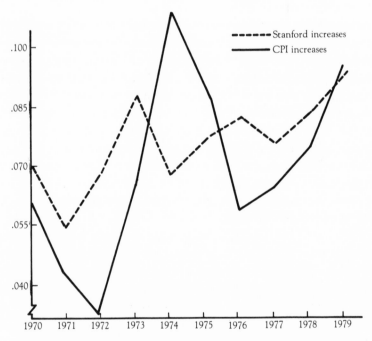

FIGURE 3.
Rates of Increase in Stanford Departments
and the Consumer Price Index

A CASE STUDY OF THE RATIONAL MODEL

importance nor funding potential proved susceptible to measurement. The former was not explicated fully enough in Miller's writings to be defined concretely; the latter, as Miller acknowledged, was difficult to extricate from a ring of circular reasoning: which came first, the decision to fund or the funds that made the decision possible?

Although only student interest and academic excellence could be measured, the analysis of these two items from the list is sufficient to test for rational decisions. If a regression equation showed that department budgets could be predicted by these two criteria, this result would establish both that Miller understood cause-effect relations in budgeting and that he had made decisions according to his expressed value system.

For each department for each of the ten years, student interest was defined as the number of instructional units taught in the year before the budget was decided minus the number taught in the previous year. The correlation between instructional units and budgets was high (.82), especially in small and average-size departments. Measuring student interest as the *change* in instructional units meant that the regression equation was unaffected by this historically strong relationship. Instead, the question was, Did the provost continually monitor his preference of student interest during his term of office?

While academic excellence could not be directly measured, its components could be identified both from the provost's writings and from traditions established by previous studies. Three such components were identified: national rank, committee representation, and research funding. These were combined through factor analysis; then this factor and the measure of student interest were fed into a policy-capturing regression equation. Both variables were found to be statistically significant as predictors of increased budget shares: departments receiving high scores on student interest or academic excellence in fact also received larger budget increases than those with low scores.

Thus, on the basis of student interest and academic excellence, the fifth criterion was satisfied.

There is substantial evidence, then, that Stanford's budgeting practices in the 1970s constituted an actual example of rational decisionmaking by an institution of higher education in an area traditionally considered political, bureaucratic, collegial, or anarchical in the character of its decisions. If budgeting, a volatile area generally thought to be necessarily divisive in character, can be rationally approached, then one is encouraged to conclude that rational decisions are possible in other areas as well. The next chapter will explore the ramifications of this thesis.

CHAPTER 3

Applications of the Rational Model

Unfortunately, it is not possible for an administrator to say, "Tomorrow we will begin to make rational decisions according to the rational formula. We will state our values, consider alternatives simultaneously, centralize the decisionmaking process, project the consequences, and verify the correlation between values and choices." The organizational situation and the decision situation must first be investigated to determine whether they will support a rational process.

Organizational Situation

Before rational decisions can be a probable outcome of the decisionmaking process, the values of the institution as a whole must be defined, a sense of stability must be present, and the power structure within the institution must be understood.

Values

The values of a college or university are traditionally expressed in its statement of mission and accompanying goals. Some administrators feel that the effort that goes into the formulation of this document is largely wasted, because they know what their college is supposed to do without stating its mission in exact words. Frequently the effort is in fact wasted, because the statements that emerge are too vague to give real guidance to those who need specific directives as bases for decisionmaking and performance evaluation. In order to serve as an adequate basis for rational decisions, mission and goals documents must exhibit two characteristics that may seem contradictory but are not: they must be concrete enough to yield actual guidance, and they must be broad enough to provide that guidance in every area it is needed.

Concreteness is essential both for choosing between alternatives and for evaluating the choice. To answer the question, "On what grounds shall faculty be evaluated for promotion?" a college will not find the statement that its goal is "to maintain an able faculty" very helpful. However, expanding the statement to read, "To maintain an able faculty of scholars with a commitment to excellent teaching of undergraduate students," provides a directive for choosing and for evaluating.

Breadth, in the sense of covering many areas, is also an essential feature of mission and goals documents, because decisions that college and university administrators make are extremely diverse. They may range from the purely financial (Shall we rent the stadium to the Panthers?) through the academic (Shall we adopt a decimal grading system?) to the moral (Shall we expel all students who cheat?) and the behavioral (Shall we create a program to discourage use of drugs in the dorms?). Participants involved in these decisions need a statement of values that will embrace this diversity and give special guidance in each of these situations.

Finally, values need to be prioritized in the mission and goals documents, to guide such decisions as, Shall we stress academic excellence or broad participation by disadvantaged students?

APPLICATIONS OF THE RATIONAL MODEL

The administrator who wishes to decide this issue rationally can then use the document as a basis not only for deciding but also for defending the decision. When priorities are not stated, decisions that involve differing values tend to be decided by non-rational processes.

Often it takes a good deal of time and effort to produce any mission or goals document, let alone a concrete one that many people can agree on. Immediate effects can be achieved without going through this process if the president is able to put into a few specific words the aspects of existing mission statements that he or she plans to emphasize. This is essentially what Provost Miller did with his four criteria for judging academic programs. These statements of emphasis should start with the president, but other top executives can then use them as a context within which to make specific goal statements for their areas of responsibility. But however it is produced, a clear statement of values is needed for rational decisionmaking.

Stability

Rational decisionmaking also needs a sense of stability, a sense that the institution will continue and is, moreover, worth the effort its members must undertake to ensure that it does continue. In a time of scarcity, some administrators may believe that this is an impossible task. I maintain that, even without an immediate change in the balance sheet, a rational administration can create stability and confidence. People feel most comfortable with decisions that are consistent with their expectations, and that also give them a sense of what the future is intended to bring. Furthermore, since everyone in a troubled institution realizes that a change in direction is needed, this may be the ideal time to pursue the rational model.

An example of the value of stability and the means of attaining it was presented to me earlier this year when I asked the presi-

Ellen Earle Chaffee

dent of a struggling liberal-arts college if I might visit and evaluate the college's situation. He hesitated a moment and then said, "Personally, I'd love to have an outside evaluation. But in the eight months since I've taken over, I've spent practically every waking moment reassuring everyone around here that this school and the values it represents deserve to survive and will survive. That confidence is finally catching on: we're going through a real spiritual regrowth, and in the long run we could come out stronger than we've ever been. Under the circumstances, I don't think I want to risk anything that might interrupt this process. But call me next year."

This administrator brought about an attitude change that was clearly value oriented. I certainly will call him next year, and while I do not expect miracles, I believe I may find a campus that exhibits more stability than some of those I have visited that shifted their values according to all demands of the environment rather than responding only in ways congruent with the values of the institution.

Consistency

In addition to prior values and a sense of stability, the institutional community needs an organization that operates consistently and in which the power structure is clearly understood. People at every level need to know how the system works and who the major players are so they can act effectively to advance their individual goals in the context of the institution's goals.

To people who do not understand the system, power may seem to be extended mysteriously, like lightning from the hands of Jove. Suddenly the history department is authorized to fill a position in modern American history; just as suddenly, that authority is rescinded. In fact, the funding and the recision of funding may be consistent with a centrally defined policy based on values. But if that is not the perception of those affected by the recision, both decisions may seem capricious.

APPLICATIONS OF THE RATIONAL MODEL

Just as writers and speakers must consider their audiences' needs as well as their own desires for expression, decisionmakers must consider their decisions from the viewpoints of those affected by them. Unless both the substance and the process of a decision are clear to those it affects, it will be regarded as yet another instance of Jovian unpredictability. The result is cynicism, which may be the most serious problem administrators face today. Eventually, I believe, cynicism from within may prove a greater threat to higher-education institutions in the 1980s than conditions imposed from without.

How can cynicism be avoided? Individual members of the institutional community must participate enough to feel that they have a stake in the institution, that the institution bases its decisions on values that are generally accepted and clearly stated, and that the bases of decisions are consistently enforced. These conditions not only decrease the likelihood of cynicism but also promote rationality in specific decision situations.

The Decision Situation

An organization's capacity to deal effectively with specific decisions depends on the ability of its administrators to analyze the decision, to assess its impact, and to understand both the complexity and the fluidity inherent in most organizational situations. In addition to determining what model will be used in the situation, decisionmakers must ask who will be affected by the decision, what kind of decision it is, and who should be involved in making it.

Model

The applicability of different models to specific situations has been dealt with in detail in chapter 1. Having examined the rational model more closely in chapter 2, we may now wish to

Ellen Earle Chaffee

ask, In what specific decisions is the rational model applicable? The answer is, Whenever the most important aspect of decision-making is to match a choice with fundamental objectives. Matching a choice with objectives is frequently, but not always, desired. Although the faculty probably want an effective and efficient leader (their objective), they do not hold a competition to see who best fits their criteria. A more fundamental premise for this decision in most cases is the will of the plurality of faculty members: the value of consensus overrides the importance of attaining the objective. On the other hand, when achieving the objective is the overriding concern, then the rational model, with its centralized decisionmaking authority, is usually more effective.

Yet the rational model has traditionally been considered less compatible than the collegial with the idea of a university, primarily because of its centralized approach. Ever since that master of English prose John Henry Newman defined this idea in terms of an idyllic, Socratic society engaged in the search for truth, group decisionmaking has been generally accepted by faculty as the modus operandi for a university. And since most college administrators come from the faculty, collegiality remains the accepted model. The fact that today's $60-billion-a-year higher-education enterprise bears little resemblance to Newman's group of earnest truthseekers has not changed, and probably will not change, this preference.

Furthermore, not only in higher education but also in business, group participation and consensus building in decision-making is becoming widely preferred to a centralized process from which some members of the group feel excluded. Numerous articles and books have recently appeared on Theory Z, the Japanese management style in which decisions are made only by consensus among all affected parties. Research studies show that organizations that practice decentralization reap such rewards as high morale, high productivity, and even superior financial performance. (See bibliography, Centralization/Decentralization. Note that these studies do not consider which decision model is in use.)

Given this predilection for decentralization, it would seem that the rational model, which requires centralization, cannot be used by an effective higher-education administrator. However, if centralization/decentralization is viewed as a flexible, rather than a static arrangement, both centralized authority and broad consensus are possible.

Centralization/Decentralization

Centralization and decentralization are generally thought to designate the opposite ends of a continuum that ranges from one person at or near the top of the hierarchy making the decision (centralization) to a person or group at or near the action level making the decision (decentralization). This is the classic, formal definition of the centralization/decentralization (C/D) continuum. But the C/D question is not simply a matter of pinpointing authority: other factors are involved that do not lend themselves to linear or hierarchical interpretation, such as breadth of participation and numbers of administrative versus non-administrative people involved. Because of these factors, the administrator need not give away the authority to make a decision in order to change the C/D of a situation. For example, to decentralize the allocation of operating budget funds, one might broaden the participation of individuals outside central administration, either by soliciting more input from department heads regarding their own areas or by adding a faculty task force. Broadening participation in this way does not require changing the allocation of authority. But when done in good faith—that is, when decisionmakers honestly listen to and take account of what others have to say—it can shift the process toward decentralization.

Ellen Earle Chaffee

Because of these fluid possibilities for altering the C/D balance, I have devised a simple figure using concentric circles, rather than the more common hierarchical pyramid, to represent decisionmaking contexts. The core area of figure 4 contains the set of individuals who participate most in the decision, while the outer area contains those who are directly or indirectly affected by it (more circles could be added, showing that those closest to the core are the most directly affected). To the extent that this outer group participates, the boundary between the two areas becomes blurred. Moreover, as the examples show, a group such as faculty may occupy the outer circle vis-à-vis administration in a C-type decision (how parking space will be allocated) and the inner circle in an E-type decision (how many students will be admitted to the doctoral program in biology).

Can an E-type decision, in which decisionmaking authority is vested in a subunit of the institution, be rational? I believe it can be if it is motivated by the desire to match the consequences of the chosen alternative with the values of the institution as a whole. The biology department may function as a microcosm of central administration in admitting doctoral students. It would be inefficient for central administration to be involved in this decision situation unless it caused problems for the university as a whole. If the biology department expanded its doctoral program in disproportion to the goals of the university, central administration could exercise its unused but understood prerogative to move into the inner circle and correct the imbalance. But on a day-to-day basis, assuming that a sense of consistency makes the rational process possible at all levels of the organization, a decision made by a subunit could be completely independent of central administration and at the same time perfectly rational for the organization as a whole.

A question remains. Since central administration does not want simply to play the role of troubleshooter, dealing with problems after they occur, how does it decide when and to what

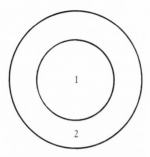

KEY: Each area can be interpreted in several ways, depending on the decision.
For example:

DECISION A: Shall we recommend a merger to the trustees?
  1 = president/top executives
  2 = faculty, staff, students, alumni, creditors

DECISION B: Is the operating budget acceptable?
  1 = governing board/legislature
  2 = each level of budget manager within the college

DECISION C: How shall we allocate parking space?
  1 = chief traffic officer
  2 = users of parking lots

DECISION D: Shall we recommend a new set of course requirements?
  1 = department or faculty senate
  2 = students, registrar, admissions officer

DECISION E: How many students will be admitted to the doctoral program in
  biology?
  1 = department faculty
  2 = biology undergraduates, financial-aid office, other administrators

FIGURE 4.

**Some Contexts For
Centralization/Decentralization**

extent it should be involved in a decision? The answer to this
question lies in an analysis of the decision itself.

Ellen Earle Chaffee

Strategic, Tactical, and Operational Decisions

While decisions may be categorized in many ways, a method that relates well to the C/D question and to rational decision-making is to apply the terms "strategic," "tactical," and "operational."

Strategic decisions, according to Hambrick (1980), (1) guide the organization in its relationship to its environment, (2) affect the internal structure and process of the organization, and (3) substantially affect the organization's performance. These decisions establish the major parameters for organizational effort and generally answer the question, What are we doing or going to do? *Tactical* decisions derive from strategic decisions and help answer the question, How are we going to do it? Through these decisions, activities are integrated and priorities are established. *Operational* decisions are still more narrow and specific, establishing procedures and answering the question, Who will do what? Examples of the three types are shown in table 6.

Both decision theory and common sense have suggested that authority to make strategic decisions should be centralized in top administration, that authority to make operational decisions should be decentralized to the affected subunits, and that the authority to make tactical decisions may appropriately vary from one situation to another. However, recent research studies have concluded that in certain strategic situations broad participation can be extremely valuable and may indeed be essential. This is particularly true when a new strategic decision is made, since the input of the people affected helps not only to produce the best informed decision possible but also to win understanding and acceptance for the decision once it is made. Additionally, in the case of new strategy, central administration should be concerned with implications at the tactical and operational levels. In other words, traditional theory, which suggests that *only* management should be concerned with strategy and that management should

TABLE 6

Illustrations of Strategic, Tactical, and Operational Decisions

Type of Decision	Summer Session	Central Purchasing	New School	Tenure Control
Strategic	Shall we initiate a summer session?	Shall central purchasing be required?	Shall we create a school of business?	Shall we freeze tenure opportunities?
Tactical	Must all departments offer courses?	Is equipment to be included?	Will it offer graduate and under-graduate courses?	Will any departments be exempt?
Operational	Which courses will depart-ment X offer?	Will it apply to orders for less than $500?	Will it accept part-time students?	Who will monitor the vital signs to alert us when the freeze goal is accomplished?

be concerned with strategy *only*, has been found in practice to be inadequate.

On the other hand, central administration must be involved in every strategic decision: it is difficult to imagine an exception to this rule. It also seems evident that all strategic decisions can be rational decisions, even though nonrational elements may be involved. For instance, the strategic decision, How aggressive shall we be in soliciting funds from the state legislature? will probably require political action for its implementation, but the decision itself may be rationally made; that is, it may be made on the basis of matching choice with the objectives of the university. Having identified the decision as strategic and therefore requiring the involvement of central administration, and having asked who will be affected by the decision, how does an administrator know when and to what extent outside participation is necessary?

Ellen Earle Chaffee

To begin at the bottom of the participation scale, participation should be most limited when the decision is urgent (a response is needed to a sudden policy shift by the legislature), when it is not important (noncontroversial data on the college is requested), when the grounds on which it is made depend wholly on specialized expertise (completion of a government survey requires interpretation of a technical term), or when the decisionmaker does not intend to pay serious attention to the contributions of the participants (the decision has already been made to eliminate the communications department; to pretend to involve members of the department in the decision—potentially a most harmful mistake—will waste the administrative staff's time and will only cause further resentment among the department members).

In the middle of the participation spectrum lie decisions that may be discussed by the people affected or by central administration or jointly, with the clear understanding that the decision-making authority rests with the administration. In joint-decision situations, the proportion of administrative staff to other participants will be high when the staff has the expertise needed for a good decision or when the administrator wishes to assert control over the decision. The Stanford budget process is an example of this type of decision: while the decision itself was obviously centralized, it depended upon and took honest account of information from every segment of the university, since every segment was affected.

Because of its widespread implications, budgeting is obviously the manifestation of strategic rather than tactical decisions. But since not all decisions can be so neatly categorized, there is a danger that administration may classify an area as tactical, allocate it to a subunit, and then have difficulty in regaining control over it. For instance, a university president is vaguely aware of irregular recruiting practices for the basketball team but has allocated responsibility for recruiting to the athletic department. Conferences with the department head do not yield complete information or produce changed practices, and the president lacks the mechanism to intervene in the earlier stages. When the irregularities are suddenly exposed, the university is forced by its moral code to cancel the entire basketball program, a decision that shocks and displeases everyone.

How can such damaging situations be avoided? Rather than abandoning authority to subunits when categorizing a decision area as tactical, a rationally oriented administrator will retain the means of exercising such authority, controversial as this stance will appear to academicians accustomed to the collegial approach. Such retention of authority may be useful, moreover, not just to prevent harmful situations but to preserve fluidity between strategic, tactical, and operational decisions in case these need to be reclassified.

The need to reclassify may arise either from within, as in the case of the basketball scandal, or from without. At a recent meeting I conducted for university administrators, a participant related that his legislature had become suddenly and intensively interested in a situation he had previously delegated because he considered it tactical. Because of their interest in the situation, decisions concerning it became strategic—these decisions would affect the college's relations with a critical constituency—and the president was placed in the awkward position of having to reclaim authority previously relinquished. Awkwardness may be alleviated, however, both by explaining the change of authority in terms of tactical versus strategic decisions and by establishing an understanding that classification or reclassification of a decision situation as "strategic" necessitates direct involvement by central administration.

An element of central direction should be present even at the broadest level of participation, where decisionmakers may be barely aware that they are acting as part of an organization. An individual teacher's decisions as to what texts to choose, what levels of student performance to demand, and what bases on

Ellen Earle Chaffee

which to award grades may be situations in which the teacher occupies the central circle of figure 4, the students occupy the outer circle, and the administration is nowhere to be found. Yet if the values and goals defined in the mission statement have been consistently applied throughout the organization and if they have been widely publicized in all departments, the administration will be indirectly guiding the situation. And if such normally operational decisions become strategic (a student given an "F" because of academic dishonesty sues the university), the administration will be expected to provide direct guidance and to assume ultimate responsibility.

Thus, to recapitulate, I maintain that the rational model, with its centralized locus of authority, can be well adapted to specific decision situations if the following conditions are met:

1. Administrators consider who will be affected by the decision and include this group in the decisionmaking process
2. Appropriate administrators are directly involved in all strategic decisions and are involved in tactical and operational decisions when necessary

Summary of Essential Features of the Rational Decision

I have discussed so many ramifications of the rational model that a summary may be helpful to administrators who are interested in working with it.

A rational decision situation must have these essential features:

1. A clear set of specific values or objectives, which serve as criteria for particular decisions
2. An organizational atmosphere of stability, confidence, and predictability

3. Consistency, on the part of the decisionmaker, with prior practice and with understood principles of decisionmaking within the institution

4. Provision for analyzing a particular situation as strategic, tactical, or operational and for determining whether the classification is permanent or temporary

5. Provision for determining who should make the decision, who will be affected by it, and to what degree each party should participate in the decisionmaking process

6. A mechanism for generating as many alternative solutions to the problem as possible and for presenting those alternatives for simultaneous consideration

7. A means of assessing the likelihood that a particular alternative will produce results that correspond with the value structure

8. A procedure for evaluating the degree to which such correspondence has been achieved and for feeding this evaluation back into the decision process

Advantages of Rational Decisionmaking

Having dealt with the major objections to the rational model and the preconditions and procedures necessary for its use in colleges and universities, we may wish to ask if establishment of the rational process is worth the effort involved. Who benefits? Evidence suggests that the beneficiaries are members of the institutional community, the administrator who uses the model, and the institution itself.

Rational procedures benefit the institutional community by making the decision process more predictable and satisfying than processes patterned on other models. The constant search to match alternatives with objectives gives a predictable structure and relatively predictable responses to the decision process, since the participants will at all points be guided by the question, How will this choice promote our objectives? Also, the link with objectives is itself satisfying: participants tend to feel that they have made the best possible decision whether or not they have actually done so. Further, they are more likely to support specific decisions, because they believe in the process by which these decisions are made. Finally, if the Stanford experience is an indication, using the model makes actors more proficient; this increased expertise may well improve both the quality of the decisions and the attitude of the institutional community toward the decision process.

The rational model confers both greater credibility and greater leadership capability to the administrator. For the routine decisions that make up the bulk of an administrator's work, credibility is usually assumed. But in difficult situations, particularly politically sensitive situations in which a segment of the institution can be expected to oppose a decision deemed necessary by an administrator, then credibility is a major issue. The administrator whose past decisions have been based on the political model, who has accommodated a group here and a group there in exchange for support, is defenseless against a charge of bias in the current situation. Nor does the bureaucratic model enhance an administrator's credibility: precedent alone is insufficient justification for most important decisions, and it is certainly inadequate to justify changes in policy. The collegial model is unworkable for most controversial decisions, since such decisions do not usually lend themselves to consensus. And the organized-anarchy model, because it is completely unpredictable, is the most damaging of all to an administrator's credibility. Only the administrator who understands and typically follows the rational model can use past practices to prove that the current decision is not biased but is rather a new link in a chain of decisions based on clearly defined values consistently applied. Like a tough but fair teacher, a tough but fair administrator will be accepted as credible. Further, an administrator who can show the rational basis of a decision has the opportunity actually to gain rather than lose credibility in difficult situations.

When decision processes are mixed, containing elements of several models, administrators may again gain credibility by emphasizing the rational element and downplaying the influence of other elements. Perception of political and anarchic elements is particularly damaging to an administrator's credibility, so the administrator familiar with the models will quickly spot and de-emphasize these elements. What will be emphasized are the value-related, rational aspects of a decision.

In addition to credibility, administrators gain a heightened leadership capacity from use of the rational model. Administrators who are value oriented, who think and speak in terms of these values, are perceived as persons of "vision," diplomats rather than politicians, true leaders rather than mere administrators. Rather than being perceived as analytical problem solvers, although this is often and justifiably part of the rational image, rational decisionmakers can become symbols of the goals that guide the institution. Only through persistently reiterating and applying those goals can an institution make progress toward them, since that progress so often requires very small steps taken over a long period of time.

Thus it is not only the individual members and administrator of an institution who benefit from persistent application of values and goals; the institution itself is the chief beneficiary. For while the rational model is a problem-solving model, it is this model's capacity to incorporate values in the day-to-day workings of a college or university that can accomplish the goal of all administrators: conversion of the ideal to the real. Fred Terman converted ideal "steeples of excellence" into measurable steeples of excellence at Stanford through his injection of that ideal into the decisions he made. William Miller replaced this individual process with an organizational process, setting up conditions and procedures that bore little or no resemblance to Terman's mental processes but that ensured that decisions would be made on the basis of the ideal that had guided Stanford to success.

At first glance, a particular college may seem to bear little resemblance to Stanford. Yet it, like Stanford, has important purposes to fulfill and people who are dedicated to the task of fulfillment. Success depends on keeping those purposes in full view of everyone and making each decision one more step toward achieving them. This is what Stanford officials did to develop their institution from a good national university in the 1940s to an internationally respected one by the 1970s; similar developments are taking place on other campuses today. Ten years ago, I am told, it was common practice for professors at the University of Colorado to downgrade the institution, the students, and even themselves. "We are hardly the Harvard of the West" was a phrase overheard in more than one department. Today CU is an institution that takes itself seriously—indeed, seriously enough to risk the headline "Teacher of the Year Fired," the example of a seemingly irrational decision with which this book began. Indications are that the institution is firmly committed to excellence in research and scholarship, and that it will risk other politically unpopular decisions to defend this goal in the difficult times ahead.

Your college will also face an increasing number of difficult decision situations if the present period of retrenchment continues. How will you handle them? What will you accomplish? Much of today's literature claims that the net effect of retrenchment will be improved quality in higher education. There are two ways this could happen. Due to circumstances created by poor decision practices as well as external factors, many colleges with low levels of support might close, leaving average quality improved nationwide. I prefer another scenario, however, in which a few colleges might close but many actually achieve higher quality in the face of retrenchment. The only way to reconcile improved quality with diminished resources is to assume that colleges have options they have not used before and that crises will encourage them to try those innovations.

But innovation alone will not improve quality during fiscal stress. The essential aspect of all decisions, innovative or traditional, is their relationship to the values and goals that are, after all, the only reasons for the existence of higher-education institutions. Administrators who use rational decision processes strengthen that relationship and provide the grounds on that difficult decisions can be made, explained, and carried out with minimal disruption, thereby ensuring the survival both of the values of higher education and of the institutions that embody them.

The Annual Operating Budget Cycle

The figure that follows outlines the eighteen-month budget cycle used at Stanford. Although this version was taken from a 1979 publication, the same cycle is presented in the budget books for every year of the Miller administration. The four-month protocol process, shown in the text as figure 2, begins in September with the development and distribution of budget protocols. The protocol process ends in January with the review of income probabilities and expense needs, followed by the determination of budget recommendations.

Both before and after the protocol process, budgeting largely involves technical functions, performed by staff analysts. The major exception is that immediately after the protocol process the president and provost submit the recommended budget to the faculty for review and to the trustees for approval. But during the protocol process people from diverse areas with conflicting claims on resources are actively involved, and the policy decisions that will guide staff analysts for the coming year are made. This period of time is the subject of chapter 2.

Ellen Earle Chaffee

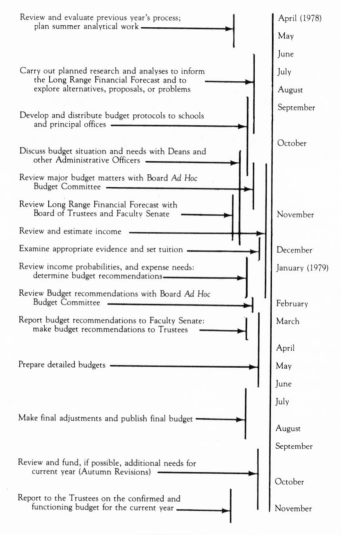

Review and evaluate previous year's process; plan summer analytical work	April (1978)
	May
	June
Carry out planned research and analyses to inform the Long Range Financial Forecast and to explore alternatives, proposals, or problems	July
	August
	September
Develop and distribute budget protocols to schools and principal offices	
	October
Discuss budget situation and needs with Deans and other Administrative Officers	
Review major budget matters with Board *Ad Hoc* Budget Committee	
Review Long Range Financial Forecast with Board of Trustees and Faculty Senate	November
Review and estimate income	
Examine appropriate evidence and set tuition	December
Review income probabilities, and expense needs: determine budget recommendations	January (1979)
Review Budget recommendations with Board *Ad Hoc* Budget Committee	February
Report budget recommendations to Faculty Senate: make budget recommendations to Trustees	March
	April
Prepare detailed budgets	May
	June
	July
Make final adjustments and publish final budget	August
	September
Review and fund, if possible, additional needs for current year (Autumn Revisions)	October
Report to the Trustees on the confirmed and functioning budget for the current year	November

FIGURE 5.

The Annual Budget Cycle

SOURCE: "Operating Budget Guidelines, 1979-1980" (Stanford: Stanford University, 1979), p. 14.

Results of the Stanford Budget Study

The results of the regression equation using the provost's priorities to predict departmental budgets are shown in table 7. Note that two of the variables in section II—budget share at time t and budget share at time $t-1$, the preceding year—are expressed as proportions. Using proportions and using the previous year's budget as a predictor accomplished several purposes in a generalized-least-squares (GLS) regression: (1) it provided data by which the GLS algorithm could calculate and correct for autocorrelation in time-series data; (2) it controlled for the budget base, which is the assumed starting point in virtually all budgeting; and (3) it made the equation dynamic, as was the process it modeled. What was left for the remaining predictor variables to explain, after controlling for the relative size of the previous year's budget, was the relative change in the current year's budget that was not due either to the budget base or to across-the-board changes.

Ellen Earle Chaffee

TABLE 7

Policy-Capturing Regression for Criterion Four

I. Regression equation
Budget$_t$ = .001 + .93 budget$_{t-1}$ + .0008 reputation + .12E-6 units change
R^2 = .9517146

II. Variables

	Mean	Std. Dev.	Budg$_{t-1}$	Correlations Reput.	Units chg.
Budget share$_t$	.033	.015	.97	.62	−.03
Budget share$_{t-1}$	.033	.015		.61	−.06
Reputation	−.96E-7	.82			−.03
Units change	−37.89	1732.17			

III. Tests for significance of contribution to R^2

Unique contribution:

Full model variables	Restricted model	Variable tested	R^2_{fm}	R^2_{rm}	F
budget share$_{t-1}$ reputation units change	budget share$_{t-1}$ units change	reputation	.951715	.94683	23.87*
budget share$_{t-1}$ reputation units change	budget share$_{t-1}$ reputation	units change	.951715	.94838	16.30*

Total contribution:

budget share$_{t-1}$ reputation	budget share$_{t-1}$	reputation	.948379	.94368	21.57*
budget share$_{t-1}$ units change	budget share$_{t-1}$	units change	.946831	.94368	14.04*

*Significant at p<.01

RESULTS OF THE STANFORD BUDGET STUDY

Variable 2, reputation, is a factor score created from three other variables by factor analysis. These three variables, selected on the basis of other research that showed what "excellence" meant to Stanford faculty members and administrators, were departmental income from grants and contracts (research), departmental representation on major university committees, and the national rank of the department from independent national surveys. Confirming the findings of the study on excellence, factor analysis revealed that these variables combined in equal proportion to create a single factor, as shown below:

	Factor Loading	Est. Communality
Share of grants and contracts	.64924	.24395
Share of committee members	.63929	.23880
National rank, inversely scored	−.63474	.23638

The factor score, which explained 41 percent of the total variance in the three variables, was used as a measure of a department's reputation for excellence, changing in each of the 10 years as the department's research funds and committee service changed. The number of departments in the study was reduced to 24 for this analysis, since 14 departments were in disciplines for which no national ranks have been calculated.

The third predictor variable is the number of credit hours taught by a department in year t-1 minus the number taught in year t-2. The reason for lagging this variable for one additional year was that at the time budgets were made, credit hours for the current year were not yet known.

The GLS regression equation is presented in section I of table 7. We ignore the previous year's budget variable since it acted primarily as a control variable. The major issue was whether the other two variables made significant contributions toward predicting the budget at t, after controlling for budget base and incremental change. This issue is addressed in section III of the table.

Each variable was tested by means of two questions:

1. Did its absence from the equation significantly reduce the overall power of the equation R^2 to predict budget adjustments? If so, the variable made a significant, unique contribution to the equation.

2. Did the variable make a significant contribution to R^2 after controlling for the previous year's budget? If so, the total contribution of the variable was not fully absorbed by its contribution to the budget of the previous year. As section III shows, the F statistic for both tests and both variables was significant at $p < .01$. These tests were chosen over customary statistical tests that rely on estimates of standard error, because the study dealt with a population, so it incorporated no sampling error.

BIBLIOGRAPHY

References Cited

Allison, Graham T. *Essence of Decision: Explaining the Cuban Missile Crisis*. Boston: Little, Brown and Company, 1971.

Bacchetti, Raymond F. Stanford University, Stanford, California. Academic Planning Office Seminar, 16 October 1978.

"California Regents Approve New Admissions Standards," *The Chronicle of Higher Education*, 30 June 1982, p. 2.

Chaffee, Ellen E. "The Role of Rationality in University Budgeting." Paper presented at the annual meeting of the American Institute for Decision Sciences, San Francisco, November 1982.

Cohen, Michael D., and March, James G. *Leadership and Ambiguity: The American College President*. New York: McGraw-Hill, 1974.

Hambrick, Donald C. "Operationalizing the Concept of Business-Level Strategy in Research." *Academy of Management Review* 5 (October 1980):567-75.

Hills, Frederick S., and Mahoney, Thomas A. "University Budgets and Organizational Decision Making." *Administrative Science Quarterly* 23 (September 1978):454-65.

Miller, William F. Stanford University, Stanford, California. Letter to Dean Williams Kays, School of Engineering, 3 June 1975.

Ellen Earle Chaffee

_____ . Stanford University, Stanford, California. Letter to Richard W. Lyman, President, 5 October 1971.

"Operating Budget Guidelines, 1979-80." Stanford University, Stanford, California, 1979.

Pfeffer, Jeffrey, and Moore, William. "Power and Politics in University Budgeting: A Replication and Extension." *Administrative Science Quarterly* 25 (December 1980):637-53.

Pfeffer, Jeffrey, and Salancik, Gerald R. "Organizational Decision Making as a Political Process: The Case of a University Budget." *Administrative Science Quarterly* 19 (June 1974):135-51.

Poulton, Nick L. "Impacts of Planning Activities in Research Universities: A Comparative Analysis of Five Institutional Experiences." Ph.D. dissertation, University of Michigan, 1979.

Decision Models

Rational Model

Cyert, Richard M., and March, James G. *A Behavioral Theory of the Firm.* Englewood Cliffs, N.J.: Prentice-Hall, 1963.

Diesing, Paul. *Reason in Society: Five Types of Decisions and Their Social Conditions.* Urbana: University of Illinois Press, 1962; Greenwood Press, 1976.

Hartwig, Richard. "Rationality and the Problems of Administrative Theory." *Public Administration* 56 (Summer 1978):159-79.

BIBLIOGRAPHY

Keen, Peter G. W., and Scott-Morton, Michael S. *Decision Support Systems: An Organizational Perspective.* Reading, Mass.: Addison-Wesley, 1978.

Kramer, Fred A. "Policy Analysis as Ideology." *Public Administration Review* (September/October 1975):509-17.

Mann, Dale. *Policy Decision-Making in Education: An Introduction to Calculation and Control.* New York: Teachers College Press, 1975.

March, James G. "Bounded Rationality, Ambiguity, and the Engineering of Choice." *The Bell Journal of Economics* 9 (Autumn 1978):587-608.

Nutt, Paul C. "Models for Decision Making in Organizations and Some Contextual Variables Which Stipulate Optimal Use." *Academy of Management Review* 2 (April 1976):84-98.

Pondy, Louis R. "Toward a Union of Rationality and Intuition in Managerial Action." Working paper, University of Illinois, Urbana, April 1982.

Quade, E. S. *Analysis for Public Decisions.* New York: American Elsevier, 1975.

Regan, D. E. "Rationality in Policy Making: Two Concepts Not One." *Long Range Planning* 11 (October 1978):83-88.

Schlesinger, James R. "Uses and Abuses of Analysis." In *American Defense and Detente*, pp. 286-99. Edited by Eu Rosi. New York: Dodd, Mead and Company, 1973.

Ellen Earle Chaffee

Simon, Herbert A. "Rational Decision-Making in Business Organizations." *American Economic Review* 69 (September 1979):493-513.

———. *Administrative Behavior: A Study of Decision-Making Processes in Administrative Organization.* New York: Free Press, 1976.

———. "A Behavioral Model of Rational Choice." *Quarterly Journal of Economics* 69 (February 1955):99-118.

Stein, Janice Gross, and Tanter, Raymond. *Rational Decision-making: Israel's Security Choices, 1967.* Columbus, Ohio: Merson Center of the Ohio State University Press, 1974.

Weil, Herman M. "Can Bureaucracies Be Rational Actors? Foreign Policy Decision-Making in North Vietnam." *International Studies Quarterly* 19 (December 1975):432-68.

Collegial Model

Keeton, Morris. *Shared Authority on Campus.* Washington, D.C.: American Association for Higher Education, 1971.

Millett, John D. *Decision Making and Administration in Higher Education.* Kent, Ohio: Kent State University Press, 1968.

Bureaucratic Model

Downs, A. *Inside Bureaucracy.* Boston: Little, Brown and Company, 1967.

Weber, Max. *The Theory of Social and Economic Organizations.* Translated by A. M. Henderson. Edited by Talcott Parsons. New York: Free Press, 1947.

BIBLIOGRAPHY

Organized Anarchy

Cohen, Michael D., and March, James G. *Leadership and Ambiguity: The American College President.* New York: McGraw-Hill, 1974.

March, James G., and Olsen, Johan P. *Ambiguity and Choice in Organizations.* Bergen, Norway: Universitetsforlaget, 1976.

Political Model

Baldridge, J. Victor. *Power and Conflict in the University.* New York: John Wiley & Sons, 1971.

Foster, Julian S. F. "A Political Model for the University." *Educational Record* 49 (Fall 1968):435-43.

Lindblom, C. E. "The Science of 'Muddling Through'." *Public Administration Review* 19 (Spring 1959):78-88.

March, James G. "The Power of Power." In *Varieties of Political Theory,* pp. 39-70. Edited by David Easton. Englewood Cliffs, N.J.: Prentice-Hall, 1966.

Pfeffer, Jeffrey. *Power in Organizations.* Marshfield, Mass.: Pitman Publishing, 1981.

Salancik, G. R., and Pfeffer, J. "The Bases and Use of Power in Organizational Decision Making: The Case of a University." *Administrative Science Quarterly* 19 (December 1974):453-73.

Tonn, Joan C. "Political Behavior in Higher Education Budgeting." *Journal of Higher Education* 49 (November/December 1978):575-87.

Ellen Earle Chaffee

Model Comparisons

Allison, Graham T. *Essence of Decision: Explaining the Cuban Missile Crisis*. Boston: Little, Brown and Company, 1971.

Dressel, Paul L. *Administrative Leadership*. San Francisco: Jossey-Bass, 1981.

George, Alexander L. *Towards a More Soundly Based Foreign Policy*. Washington, D.C.: Government Printing Office, 1975.

Centralization and Decentralization

Mortimer, Kenneth P., and McConnell, T. R. *Sharing Authority Effectively, Chapter 9: Decentralization and Centralization*. San Francisco: Jossey-Bass, 1978.

Vroom, Victor H., and Yetton, Philip W. *Leadership and Decision-Making*. Pittsburgh, Pa.: University of Pittsburgh Press, 1973.

C/D and Organizational Condition

Bragg, J. E., and Andrews, I. Robert. "Participative Decision Making: An Experimental Study in a Hospital." In *The Study of Organizations*, pp. 531-36. Edited by Daniel Katz, Robert L. Kahn, and J. Stacy Adams. San Francisco: Jossey-Bass, 1980.

Lawler, Edward E., III; Hall, Douglas T.; and Oldham, Greg R. "Organizational Climate: Relationship to Organizational Structure, Process and Performance." *Organizational Behavior and Human Performance* 11 (February 1974):139-55.

BIBLIOGRAPHY

Neghandi, A. R., and Reimann, B. C. "Task Environment, Decentralization and Organizational Effectiveness." *Human Relations* 26 (February 1973):203-14.

Pennings, Johannes M. "Dimensions of Organizational Influence and Their Effectiveness Correlates." *Administrative Science Quarterly* 21 (December 1976):688-99.

Reimann, Bernard C. "Dimensions of Structure in Effective Organizations: Some Empirical Evidence." *Academy of Management Science* 17 (December 1974):693-708.

Stagner, Ross. "Corporate Decision Making: An Empirical Study." *Journal of Applied Psychology* 53 (February 1969):1-13.

C/D and Organizational Size

Baldridge, J. Victor. "College Size and Professional Freedom." *Change* (May 1973):11.

Blau, Peter. "Decentralization in Bureaucracies." In *Power in Organizations*, pp. 150-74. Edited by Mayer N. Zald. Nashville, Tenn.: Vanderbilt University Press, 1970.

Boland, Walter R. "Size, External Relations and the Distribution of Power: A Study of Colleges and Universities." In *Comparative Organizations*, pp. 428-40. Edited by Wolf V. Heydebrand. Englewood Cliffs, N.J.: Prentice-Hall, 1973.

Child, John. "Predicting and Understanding Organization Structure." *Administrative Science Quarterly* 18 (June 1973): 168-85.

Ellen Earle Chaffee

Hinings, C. R., and Lee, G. L. "Dimensions of Organization Structure and Their Context: A Replication." *Sociology* 5 (January 1971):83-93.

C/D and Organizational Complexity

Grinyer, Peter H., and Yasai-Ardekani, Masoud. "Dimensions of Organizational Structure: A Critical Replication." *Academy of Management Journal* 23 (September 1980):405-21.

Hage, Jerald, and Aiken, Michael. "Relationship of Centralization to Other Structural Properties." *Administrative Science Quarterly* 12 (June 1967):72-91.

C/D and Intraorganizational Communication

Hage, Jerald; Aiken, Michael; and Marrett, Cora Bagley. "Organization Structure and Communication." *American Sociology Review* 36 (October 1971):860-71.

Lincoln, James R., and Zeitz, Gerald. "Organizational Properties from Aggregate Data: Separating Individual and Structural Effects." *American Sociological Review* 45 (June 1980):391-408.

Mileti, Dennis S.; Gillespie, David F.; and Eitzen, D. Stanley. "Structure and Decision Making in Corporate Organizations." *Sociology and Social Research* 63 (July 1979):723-44.

C/D and Environmental Uncertainty

Duncan, Robert B. "Multiple Decision Making Structures in Adapting to Environmental Uncertainty: The Impact on Organizational Effectiveness." *Human Relations* 26 (March 1973):273-91.

BIBLIOGRAPHY

Hrebiniak, Lawrence, G., and Snow, Charles C. "Industry Differences in Environmental Uncertainty and Organizational Characteristics Related to Uncertainty." *Academy of Management Journal* 23 (December 1980):750-59.

Pennings, Johannes M. "The Relevance of the Structural-Contingency Model for Organizational Effectiveness." *Administrative Science Quarterly* 20 (September 1975):393-410.

Robey, Daniel. "Computers and Management Structure." In *The Study of Organizations*, pp. 33-42. Edited by Daniel Katz, Robert L. Kahn, and J. Stacy Adams. San Francisco: Jossey-Bass, 1980.

The NCHEMS
Executive Overview Series

Each year, the NCHEMS Executive Overview subscription will elucidate a general theme. The theme for 1982 is Decisions and Decision Information.

The central problem of sound decisionmaking in higher education is how to arrive at informed, forward-looking decisions—decisions that maximize institutional effectiveness while minimizing the negative impacts of financial stress, shifting program demand, and changing clientele. Established decision processes usually were not intended to cope with a quick succession of decisions involving far-reaching change. Similarly, conventional sources and channels of information often are inadequate to meet today's decision needs.

Each Executive Overview in the 1982 Subscription will explore some key aspects of the administrator's decision responsibility.

The 1982 Executive Overview Subscription includes six books in the series, plus a bonus book for subscribers. The cost is $60, or $70 outside the continental United States.

The books are also available individually at $10.00 each plus 50¢ per copy for shipping and handling.

The 1982 NCHEMS Executive Overview Series:

Data and Information for Executive Decisions in Higher Education By Dennis P. Jones

Program Review in Higher Education: Within and Without By Robert J. Barak

Rational Decisionmaking in Higher Education By Ellen Earle Chaffee

How to Acquire and Use Student-Outcomes Information By Peter T. Ewell

Comparative Data in Higher Education By Paul Brinkman and Jack Krakower

The Effective Use of Management Consultants in Higher Education By Jana B. Matthews

Bonus for Subscribers—

A Survival Kit for Invisible Colleges, 2nd ed. By Norbert J. Hruby, President, Aquinas College

Order Form

Six Books in the Series plus a Bonus for Subscribers!

☐ I wish to subscribe to the NCHEMS 1982 Executive Overview Subscription ($60 for one year, $70 for one year outside the continental United States)

Name _____ Title _____

Department _____ Institution _____

Address _____ City _____ State _____ Zip _____

☐ Payment Enclosed   ☐ Charge Institutional Purchase Order #_____
(Please make checks payable to NCHEMS)   (Enclose Purchase Order with this form)

☐ I do not wish to subscribe, but I would like to receive the 1982 Executive Overviews listed below at $10.00 each:

QTY.	TITLE	PRICE
	Plus 50¢ per book for shipping and handling	
	Total	

RETURN TO:
NCHEMS Publications Department / P.O. Drawer P / Boulder, Colorado 80302
or call (303) 497-0390

85